MW01199478

Life

to

ME!

****EDITED BY: TOREY WILLIAMS****

ISBN 978-0-9787439-7-0

Publisher By:
DBROCKMAN PUBLISHING,
Post Office Box 173208
Tampa, Florida 33672
Local Phone (813) 390-1556
Info@dbrockmansr.info
dbpublisher@yahoo.com

Life To Me!

Introduction

Allow me to thank you for responding to me. It's nice to meet you as well. Let me tell you a little about myself. My name is Renard O. Bennett. I'm from a place called Belle Glade, Florida, about 30 miles away from West Palm Beach in the same county. If you have ever been to West Palm or South Florida period you know it's beautiful. I'm currently located in Columbia, South Carolina. I have always traveled since I was young, my siblings and I. It was a plus because it gave me the advantage of seeing how others from different environments viewed life, and ever since then I've been on the go.

I was educated at a Columbia H.B.C.U by the name of Allen University, and **it** has to receive recognition for my excellence. **It** helped me achieve this goal I have attained today and will be responsible for many more accomplishments in the future. I still haven't received my degree from college yet but I will go back and finish up. "Don't start nothing up and don't finish" is what my grandfather always told me. I have to do for my family if not for myself. The other reason is I have three more classes to take before I finish my degree in English. I'll get there. I can remember one day in class my professor was discussing an author's poem and I asked, "How can you be a writer and have run on sentences in your poems?" She replied, "When you are a good writer you can get away with things like that." So I said, "I'm a good writer." She told me that I wasn't good and she challenged me to become better.

I admit that I was never was a person to display my talents. Pretty much I was lazy. So the class had an assignment to write a sequel of the story Lincoln West by Gwen Lynne Brook. I got home that day and rewrote this amazing end to this story and read it to the class the following class period. She was impressed, my professor of course. It was so shocking that no one in the class wanted to go after me. That is when I realized I had a gift with a pen and a piece of paper. This is my first book, but expect more to come from me. Expect to see me as a role model, a man that lives for right and man who honors reality.

This book talks about the acknowledgement of self. I feel you must know yourself in order to know others. This is more like a new beginning to my life. As I grow stronger in the society with a positive mindset I will display more of my thoughts, but for now I will give civilization only a sample of my soul.

The Sequel to the Life of Lincoln West

Silence, darkness, flashing lights from the stormy weather attacks my room. Rain harasses my window pane. I'm disgusted with myself. How could I bring myself to this? They made me do this. Over and over I tell myself that **they** made me the animal that I am. **They're** the creator and I'm the creation.

Why must I take it this far? Why I ask? Why! Couldn't we just resolve our problems differently? We should just have talked it over. Life then may have been better. But NO, they wouldn't listen to me. See what happens for not listening to me? Not loving me? Not wanting me?

God, what have I done? As the blood races down my uneasy flesh on to the surface of my home, my wretched home, there's an unpleasant silence that overcomes my surroundings. A stressful pain tortures my heart. As I struggle with this excruciating pain, I find myself in a trance.

Standing face to face with the destroyer, I envision my youthful years. They never wanted me, they never accepted me. Now years later it results in this. As my body temperature begins to rise blood, tears and sweat run from my weary face. Why me? Oh Lord why me...I just wanted to be loved, that's all! I just wanted to be loved. Mama, I just wanted to be loved. Daddy, I wanted to be loved. I just wanted to be loved, I just wanted to be... BOOM!

Silence, darkness, flashing lights from the stormy weather attacks my room. Blood drips from my window pane.

My Eyes Start Twitching
My Toes Start Burning

Relaxed, lying in my bed, enjoying the voices that come from the television. I have my head leaned back against the head board, dazed in a light sleep. The effects of marijuana steal me. In a dreamy world, I vision me. A King, a Rebel, Master. I control all elements. Love is me, Peace is me, Life is me.

Just like that it hits me. A scorching heat increases my body temperature. Hot cramps rush thru me as if in punishment. I begin to toss and turn, trying to position myself into a comfortable spot in my resting place. Uneasily, the cramps continue to roam my burning body. My mind then began to focus on another. Not expecting this guess. Certainly unwanted, it ravages me. Pain is a part of me, and it becomes a ruthless tormentor.

I then envision life, an unbearable place. A master destroyed, a rebel conquered, a kingdom fallen. Weeping sorrowfully for my downfalls I find myself at my knees asking God's forgiveness. Then you appear in the midst of a bright light, only noticeable as a figure. As I place my arm against my startled face, blocking my eyes from this amazing light that surrounds me, you touch me. Cold chills begin to arrest my soul. Stunted by this unique touch, I become dysfunctional. Forced to detach my arms away from my face, I saw yours...

A vision I never had before, beauty at its greatest form. With a smile whiter then snow, a colored face as pure as the Virgin Mary and hair rich like gold. You spoke, I trembled. You laughed, I trembled. You silence yourself, I still trembled.

Leaving my dreamy world, in fast breaths I become content with our world. Opening my eyes, still placed in my comfort zone, the television catches my attention for a brief second. Out of nowhere I hear your amazing voice, and it motivates me to become the light I saw in you. Then you silenced yourself. I ponder to myself, where did you go? I'm waiting on an answer from you, you never replied.

Then out of the blue you laugh, and then I smile. You let me know you will never leave me nor forsake me. A mutual understanding we possess in one another. Physically, Mentally, and Spiritually we are one. All aspects in life are inclined in us. Your Love, Respect, and Honor I am grateful for. When I see you again I'm hoping we meet on good terms. I just have one request. Please, don't make my eyes twitch and my toes burn.

You

In my room, staring out the window and all I do is think of you. But who are you? I ask myself, "Who are you"? When will see you? When will I meet you? All I do is imagine you. A beautiful mahogany complexion, curves as if you were conceived on drawing paper, gorgeous long black hair. Light brown eyes that glow along with your pearled smile, one that brightens up the world we exist in, and a red silk grown that covers you from your breasts down.

As I reach for you to grace you in my arms, intending to never let you go, you disappear. I question myself? "How can I let something so wonderful leave my presence?" I then return to myself, figuring you are a figment of my imagination.

Then a soft voice speaks. "She's there and you will see her again, let time take its place. She's your strong backbone, lifting you up when no one else will. She pushes you to strive for your dreams and goals, remaining in your life for better or worse. The precious one you gaze at when she's fast asleep, thanking God for this gift of joy."

You laugh with me. You cry with me. "But who are you"? I ask myself. My Nubian Queen, I will cook for you while cleaning you. Massage your thoughts while caressing your feelings. Go to the deepest cave for you, climb the tallest mountain for you. You give me hope, you give me honor, you give me life. Yet I still ask myself, "Who are you?"

You are every man's dream, but only for me. You are the true definition of a dime piece. Being soul mates we do face conflict, but the love we possess in our soul accepts no negativity. Our love grows daily as one mind, one body and one soul. We will live together forever happy. No doubts, our life is secured. But still I ask myself, "Who are you?"

There's A Person

Take a little girl...innocent, humble, patient. Her life consists of peace. Happy! She sees no evil. Her lifestyle only accepts positive emotions. No worries. She enjoys everyday as if it was her only wish. She doesn't ask for the high maintenance, the only simple gifts she craves for are her desires. Having love and laughter for entertainment, the world is her play ground. She is satisfied. Now ask yourself, "Are you that person?"

Now take a little boy, Superman! He truly feels unbreakable. Tough, he enjoys the times in the flatlands, playing unorganized football with his friends. Calm, and like the little girl he's humble. A leader, his friends cling to him as they skip rocks across the pond near the country side. He never shows favoritism toward his buddies for they are one. Now are you this person?

There's a Young man, educated. He has lived up to his dreams and goals and has achieved them well. A role model, little boys scream out, "I want to be like him when I grow up." A complete gentleman, never disrespected a woman, instead motivates her to be the lady he see in her. His name is always spoken good of, makes him stand out prestigiously. Now tell me, "Are you this person"?

Ms. Lady, a woman of purity. This queen is far past a dime piece and silver dollar. She's in a league of her own. She lives more in spirit than in flesh, which makes her outer appearance more amazing. A glow, the light she possesses during the days of her life. Never a put down, but embrace for her wonderful works in society. To that gentleman she's his biggest supporter, his secured backbone. Ask yourself this question, "Are you this person"?

There's an elder gentleman. He thinks back to his youthful years and oh how he misses them so much. But he's content with life, for he's set in his old ways. Cool, calm and collected. He's too old to stress about the troubles in the world. Full of wisdom he leans back in his rocking chair on his front porch of his aged home, happily telling stories to his grandchildren of his past life and giving them a vision of society. He is preparing them for what's to come to their growing lives. This old soul has seen hard times, but he only contemplates on the joy life has given him. Tell me, "Are you this person"?

Mother, Grandmother, Big Mama. She's the centerpiece that holds her generations together. A defined woman who symbolizes love and unity through out her surroundings, she's the queen of her environment and she's asking for strength and knowledge to deal with the ways of the world. For years she struggles with pain, she still has managed not to reveal her hurt. Peaceful, as she lies down to rest her reward is paid in full. A woman of essence, this good old queen has raised good queens and kings, giving them only good and thusly solidifying her legacy. Now tell me, "Are you this person"?

Expressions

My mind wonders, my thoughts are in a rage. My expressions are in a state of mind, trying to return to my humble self. I focus on the excitement life has brought to me. Introduced to the finer things in life, at moments I feel I'm not. So I think to myself what can I do to experience the true meaning of happiness?

Then ideals come to my head. Can I save the world from hunger? Can I be a role model to that young person just as old as me? Just because I walk an elder person across a busy street does this constitute to my happiness? With a burden in mind I asked the question, how could I be better than the average man? Then a thought pops into my head. When everyone's life seems to go even my lifestyle will be odd. My life is precious, therefore it should be handled with care at all times. This treasure I possess of my own world, piece by piece. Becoming a transistor, civilization shall experience my advancement in life.

I then ask myself, how did I become this remarkable light to society? Ideals again rush my mind. I must love, for love is life itself. Is it possible I questioned myself? If one has the ability to love then one has the power to overcome the deception that defiles mankind. Providing this love to your countrymen builds security of trust in you, this makes you special because man will not put his trust in self. He will seek leadership from you.

Understand everyone is capable of seeing the light. Therefore, you must shine in the darkest places. Places where life is at it's weakest link. Where tears form a pond on harmful land, where scorned hands reach out wishing to be healed, a place where minds are slaves to negative thoughts that want to be free. You must go to these troubled places and establish your home. Good will out weigh the world's bad, saving life that it may see it's true home at the end of it's long journey someday.

So I question more, do I live my dreams? I was once told you would be a fool to dream. Does this make life non-fiction, because life at times is a dream? I also heard them say follow your dreams and see where they take you. A voice commenting on my thoughts saying your dreams are your reality, a vision that comes with assistance makes half the journey. Then I remembered a time in grade school my teacher asked me what I wanted to be when I grow up, not having full understanding of that question I answered it with a careless answer. Now that I have experience life and greatness of it, I can answer that question making a thoughtful decision.

I want to be that man that brings faith and hope to the world, providing new days for lost tomorrows, honoring the way of the peace. A new world is formed and given trust. This world is lifted knowing that this bond between me and society cannot be broken, but embraced with a joy spread through out this fertilized land. I am a man of tomorrow for I have overcome my yesterday.

A Mother's Land

Long gone a mother's land, tears falls from her face. Her heart can barely stand the pain of her lost fortune. This life she has inherited troubles her soul. She's in need of some relief, her mind is at its last normal thoughts. She's tired from physical and mental abuse.

Her body feels as if it was raped and scorned by strong hands. Blood leaks from her flesh, runs her leg, off her feet and onto her land. Bad blood flows her land. Her flesh is now free, but her soul remains a slave. Her sons and daughters have distressed her name, for they have banished her land. For centuries her land has been disturbed. She has had enough of suffering.

Out of anger she uses force, destroying life in high and low places. She cries and cries as she destroys and destroys out of hurt given to those pained and suffering, as they have given to her. She destroys and destroys it until there's nothing left to destroy. She didn't expect for life to be this way. Now lonely, the sky is her only friend. Surround by smoke in the night, she gazes into the eyes of the shiny face and she wonders what's next. She begins to search for a place abnormal to her body, mind, and soul. She finds herself on a cloudy road. Her vision becomes bright.

She has found new land. A world where the tree's give her praise, beasts greet her as royalty and the sea calms at her presence. Mother adores her new home. A place where tears flow no more, a broken heart is non-existing, pain and suffering are destroyed enemies. Her soul has been restored.

Her new sons and daughters appreciate her love as they rejoice, honoring her name. She grants them with new talents, that her children may improve her new world with these special gifts. She finds herself at amazing peace. As she walks her fertile land happiness is now her friend, and she embraces life for her world is paradise.

A Colored Man's Wish

Colored Man listen, I have been in the world and experienced pain and struggle. At times I cry to my lonely self, asking God why me? I never hear a voice in return. I was allowed to see that my wrong doing came from my own actions. I then realize it wasn't God punishing me, it was ME punishing me. I had allowed evil and wickedness to consume me.

I then thought to myself, "How can I become an earned man?" I acknowledge that prayer has always been the answer, a key that opens the door of righteousness which provides a vision of unbroken promises.

Colored Man listen, we must form unity amongst ourselves. Knowing this we can experiences paradise as a whole. Joining hand to hand, man and woman, boy and girl, rejoicing seeing that moment in a beautiful way.

Nevertheless, be deceased with the greed and envious wants of physical treasures. By accepting your treasures mentally and spiritually a mind set that offers strength, wisdom, knowledge, and maturity will educate you to live life first in mind and spirit before flesh. These are the keepers of our soul.

Honoring my mind set, it leads me to living life as a promising man.

Colored Man listen, build your home from a foundation of standards and morals. Understanding that respect must be given to self before respect is earned from others. A prestigious role model takes total dedication and focus. Not only are we living our own lives, we live someone else's life as well. Giving them hope along with faith. They are our leaders for yet to come.

Color Man Listen, we must acknowledge where our help comes from. This help comes from the heaven above. Our Father, Our Lord, Our God. He is who strengthen us. He provides our day and knows our tomorrow.

To God be a loyal and faithful servant, for anything against Him is sin and the wager of sin is death. To embrace Him is paradise.

Colored Man these words I say to you give knowledge, wisdom, maturity, peace, guidance, humbleness, success, truth and promise down a path of love that builds a foundation, that grows a tree of unity. Words that produce ripe fruits in today's civilization.

These words I know the Colored Man will abide by, because he listens.

Intro To Life To Me

As I wake up to the rays of the sun, that shine upon my face. I feel the blood pumping through my veins as I stretch and yawn. I get on my knees and pray. I thank the Lord for this day. As life began for me I ask "What should I experience? What should I accomplish"? Do I uphold the value I have set myself?

Life to Me

The rapper Lil Wayne once said, "I'm an 80's babe, a fighting nigga". I some what agree with Mr. Wayne's expression. I'm also an 80's babe and I'm fighting for the truth and justice which is proclaimed as a part of the American way. I believe that change is good. Many people may say that change varies, (meaning change could be either good or bad). I disagree with this worldly opinion. We're brought into this world developing a negative mind set. The change comes into our life when we develop a godly mind set. This allows us to be more open minded about life, having a vision which was once blinded by a narrow mindset.

It's kind of funny how we as people emphasize the things that defiles us rather than focusing on the things that cause growth in our life. We'd rather live for today instead of living for tomorrow and the day after that. We get caught up in trying to satisfy other people's wishes, which is impossible because people will always expect more from you and they will never be satisfied. You could never put your trust in self. Like other people you will always want more, leaving you never satisfied. Therefore, we must put our faith and trust in God who accepts us for what we are, then leads us to the lifestyle that he intends for us to live.

In this book, I will not criticize. I feel no man can judge another man for he is not perfect himself. I also feel it's not judging an individual if that individual is displaying his character openly. There's a saying, "practice makes perfect". I believe if you practice thinking positive, you will develop a positive outlook on life. This leads you to taking positive actions. Positive meaning good, take away one of the O's out of good and you have God, who is good all the time.

Now, it's not easy living a positive lifestyle. True indeed, there are many obstacles in the world to discourage an individual from living a grounded lifestyle. That said, I believe that if you focus on getting self right life becomes more comfortable for you. The first step to getting self right is admitting to your faults and then ceasing your mistakes.

Everyone has issues, it's just that majority of us don't know how to handle our issues and only a small portion of us do. In reference to my opinion, it's easy to judge an individual because there's no challenge there. It's difficult to help an individual because you have to use effort in providing for that individual.

I believe in doing unto others as you want them to do for you. This starts with giving respect, not demanding respect. If you respect everyone's space they have to respect your space. They may not like you, but they will respect your space. It's just when you cross paths you either become offensive, defensive or vulnerable. You become either motivated or manipulated.

In most case we become manipulated before motivated. We allow our flesh to think for us instead of respecting our soul that provides thought-through decisions. Here's an example: You and your close friend are at his crib just killing time playing video games, eating fast food and vibing to some old tunes. So times goes by and ya'll still chillin'.

All of a sudden your closest friend pulls out a Bob Marley, a.k.a the blunt. Now at this point you don't smoke and never had the desire to smoke. Your homeboy knows you don't smoke so he doesn't ask you if you want to hit the blunt. He lights his blunt, the smoke fills the air. You begin to smell the aroma from the good green as it drifts. Your mind becomes seduced by this aroma wondering how the sticky really makes you feel. Your flesh begins to desire the effect of the Bob Marley. This when you become motivated, keyword desire (want) is enough effort for motivation.

Motivation comes from both positive and negative aspects in life which are experiences. Jason Michael Garcia's book "The Hidden Truth Revealed" speaks on the word "Motivation". The book states, "Motivation is a voluntary and involuntary action." I agree. Motivation is a drive from anything that inspires you to fulfill your task. Like in my example, the aroma in the air from good green manipulated you. Fact being, you never smoked before. Becoming curious of how the blunt tastes you want to try the blunt. This is where you become motivated.

I believe we have two mindsets, a physical mindset and spiritual mindset. If you're familiar with bad and good conscience then you understand what the physical and spiritual mind set is about. Your physical mind set allows you to do what you want do, in most events it leads to reckless actions. Your spiritual mind set allows you to see your purpose before taking actions.

We all have good and bad in us. It's our personal choices that make us or break us. Which goes with the saying, "You make your own bed, and you have to lie in it". Choices are "free will". God or The Devil don't make us do anything. Both present things to us. It's up to us as to which lead we follow. This is called free will. Either we choose to do well, or we choose to do bad. Go down a straight and narrow path, or travel a rocky road. Every individual is accountable for their own actions.

People often fear other people. In most situations we often fear what controls other people. I look at Mr. Tupac Shakur. Most of society viewed him as a thug, a disappointment to civilization. Little of society saw him as a prophet, God send.

To me Mr. Shakur was God sent, never judging him according to what people made him out to be. Analyzing Mr. Shakur for myself I saw his leadership, his purpose. The passion he had for truth is now stored within me. A man that spoke with power and ambition helps me carry his torch on my journey of life, hoping to pass the torch to the next soldier who waits for me down the way. Being a part of Mr. Shakur's legacy, "He's not dead, he's yet alive". The great ones never die.

DMX once said he's here for a reason because he was supposed to be gone a long time ago. Which lead him to asking God to give him a sign, that he may walk his rightful path? Nas said, "All he need is One Mic and the world will display a moment of silence". T.I. said, "You have to constantly keep self in check, to keep self on point".

Martin Luther King said, "I have a dream that one day mankind will become whole".

When I get on my knees at night before bed or on my daily stroll around my neighborhood I often talk to God and I believe he listens. I ask God to give me wisdom, knowledge and maturity. Give me vision and strength. Prepare me for the things that will come about in this world. Help me to become connected with myself, one body, one mind, one soul. This helps me to acknowledge myself daily. I am a growing light, but as I travel this lonely road I face the hardships of life that leave my flesh torn and my mind puzzled. My soul never lets go. Therefore, the world can't consume me. While in this world I'm not of this world. Lord I ask, "Bless my loved ones as well as those who hate against me. Lord this is my prayer to you. Amen."

What we all have in common is our purpose in life. People who are going in the same direction also share the same dreams and goals. People may take different routes achieving them, but they always meet up at the same destination. This means we learn and grow from everyone. I find this to be the importance of life, the greatest education an individual can engage in.

When an elder person tells you, "When it rains it pours" this means when trouble comes it brings pain and suffering. A young child tells you "Hacuna-Matata", which means no worries because troubles don't last always. I try not to go in to the next day with yesterday's problems. To me you can't function with a rumbling mind, but to have a stable mind you have to develop a sense of direction.

I now ask the question, "What are the factors of life"? Most people may say "A stable household, a secured financial status and a strong relationship with God". I pose another question, "Which of these aspects is most important in your life?" A majority of the people that answer this question may say, "God is number one in my life." This leads to the ultimate question, "Do you give your all and all to God and his works?"

While writing this book, I had a conversation with my mother. I asked her, "What is your interpretation of the word reality?" She stated, "You could want to be good all you want to, but until you actually do good you still have a problem of wanting to be good. Just like a smoker saying, 'I want to stop smoking' or 'I'm going to stop smoking.' Until, that smoker deletes smoking from his/her life that person is still a smoker. Reality is the actual."

When I meet most people personally, engaging in a conversation with them, I often ask the question, "Where do you see yourself 5 years from now"? Most people tell me where they want to be and not where they need to be. We don't focus on the two pictures that are being presented here. The lifestyle you live now is the lifestyle that leads you to where you're going to be 5 years from now. I think we as people don't focus on what's best for us. Like I stated earlier in the book, we get caught up in our own wants, not allowing our needs to become our wants. We make up our own ways of life instead respecting life's wrongs and rights, life's laws and life's purpose for us. We have to keep in mind, "We don't ask to be here in civilization, we are chosen to be here in civilization".

As I continue to write this book I think back to the times I was happy. Believe it or not, most of my happiness came from my childhood. I remember the days with me and my friends playing sandlot football in the open fields of Belle Glade, Florida. I can remember us traveling the dirt roads of Belle Glade, jumping canal after canal for amusement. I remember birthday parties when we all gathered enjoying the fun of one another, sleepovers, road trips. Life was simple then. Now that I'm adult, life is seen differently. Everyone you played with at the playground aren't now all your friends. Time that was once stopped now ticks away, and some of the most beautiful dreams turned into nightmares.

Belle Glade, a city where strangers make you feel at home, a place where struggle is just another day. Belle Glade has always been an inspiration in my life. My friends have always been my friends, my family has always been my family, and my friends are my family.

The Muck, a place where young men catch rabbits amongst the burning cane fields chasing their dreams of being in the NFL one day. A place where a country princess makes the perfect country queen.

Belle Glade, a place that faces many stereotypes, but it's people manage to stand out across the nation. A city that emphasizes the values of life. Living by these standards and morals, Belle Glade has fixed me, not to be broken. Even if I don't remain there in body, I will always remain there in mind and spirit. This is my acknowledgement to my city, my town, my home. God bless Belle Glade.

I was raised by the saying, "A family that prays together stays together". Living by these words I have a wonderful relationship with my family. My mother has installed in me and my siblings the thought that all we have is each other. Teaching us love for each other causes our love for one another to grow daily.

My mother is a lady of essence, truth, strength, courage, real identity and so many other things. I describe my mother as devoting herself to hard work during her manageable days. She now lives by her method work smarter, not harder. What my mother has deposited in me and my siblings is hope for a better tomorrow, faith in ourselves and trust in God.

What plays in my mind while writing this section of this book is the gospel song, "I Won't Complain". Even though there are times where my family and I face our share of heartaches and pains God always shows us through, so we don't complain. This being rooted in my family my mother has done well raising men of tomorrow and a lady of today.

I believe if you train a child in a positive direction, she/he will never depart from it. This is called good parenting. Some people may say, "Good parenting is providing a roof over a child's head, putting clothes on a child's back, and providing food for a child's hunger". To me the good parenting title displays much more than those aspects.

When I become a father, the one thing I want to teach my offspring is, "Never assume, always know". This means if you aren't educated about something you are curious about knowing, either learn about it or don't deal with it at all. When you assume about something, you take a chance that can possible be an incorrect decision that's being made. However, knowing your thought is a fact gives you a better outcome of any situation.

Good parenting doesn't stop at the age of 18. We as parents have to realize that our offspring are with us until death do us part. Our children need our guidance along their life's journey. Good parenting doesn't live in the past, for those days are far gone. Living for today, mothers and fathers discover lost relationships with their youth. Good parenting is understanding and respecting your child. This starts with communicating with your child, educating your child daily about life. School doesn't start at day care, it starts from the womb. Giving this gift to your offspring, they will always respect and honor your good parenting.

The most important aspect of good parenting is a family as a whole. A lot of society lacks this gift of life. I'm also victim of a single parent home. Wanting to give my children this lifestyle I wasn't privileged to have, I strive hard to achieve this Godly goal. This is the reality of good parenting.

Love is an emotion that grows. As my mother says, "Love don't hurt, harm or abuse". Now, some of society may say different, like "There's a thin line between love and hate". I beg to differ. How is it that something with a positive background brings forth negative tension? That will make love bitter not sweet, when in actuality love is sweet. Now I believe in people and their persuaded mind's hurt, but not love.

Love is a mutual understanding, produced from the soul that builds soul mates. You must see yourself in the individual. You find companionship with them, and vice versa. In order to engage in a successful relationship with your better half you must be aware of the three C's. The C's are communication, compromising, and commitment. This builds security in the relationship you have with your significant other. This does not only apply with companionship, but with friendship and partnership as well.

In most cases, people confuse infatuation and lust for love. Infatuation being an emotion built from time, lust being an emotion built from physical aspects. In order to achieve this priceless emotion you must first love yourself. People only add to your happiness, just like people only add to your unhappiness if you are an unhappy person. You control you.

Personal growth is my purpose for writing this book. My book displays a person's growth as an act which man needs become a greater person in society. By acknowledging oneself then one can acknowledge others. This being put into action builds positive unity in our society.

Acknowledging self gives you a better judgment of what you accept in your lifestyle, allowing you to see negative before it could damage your surroundings. A majority of the things we go through in life are what we take ourselves through in life.

I often tell people, "We wake up each morning not knowing if we will reenter that bed we climbed out of, so we begin each new day taken a risk. Why add extra risk to your life? In better terms, there are things that we have no control over such as aging, death, bills and health in most cases. I feel the things we do have control over should be our main priorities such as living life in moderation, treasuring each day as if it was our last, and making our needs a necessary. This prepares our mind and soul to take a stand during the times we can't control."

I feel if you are the same person you were last year, you are not growing in life. Any time you are not growing in life you're at a stronghold in life. This leads you to becoming physically and mentally as well spiritually dead. Without personal growth life is passing you by.

I do consider myself a well-rounded individual. Having the ability to adapt to any environment I always manage to show my true character, which is a positive individual. A student and teacher to the principles of life I believe in, "What you live by, is what you die by". I heard Minister Farrakhan once say, "People hated Jesus, and if you are walking in the light of God, people will persecute you as well".

I see life as a major picture movie. God is the big man behind the scenes, only seen when the time is needed. We are the actors/actresses. Some of us have bad roles, the devil is the media and critics who insist on making our life dramatized.

Not caught up in the politics of civilization, I remain humble and wise on my daily journey in life. I fulfill my quest by learning to allow God to order my steps, then I know I will succeed on my mission that lays before me.

Leadership...I know my purpose in life is to be a national leader. Some may say, "How do you know it's your purpose to lead?" Well, in order to be a leader you must understand the concept of being a leader, qualities that I do possess.

A Leader is an individual who provides guidance to the unfortunate or mislead, helping them find their rightful path in life. A leader installs knowledge, wisdom, and maturity in individuals who wish to grow in that direction. A leader leads by example, allowing his/her good to out weight his/her bad. A leader's name should always be spoken well of, for his/her lifestyle does affect his/her congregation. In reference to the saying, "If the head is not right then body is not right".

Now leaders are presented in two forms, Motivators and Manipulators. Motivators are leaders who are concerned about people lifestyles, helping them to overcome their life's burdens. Manipulators are presented as leaders who expose individual's weaknesses by draining them physically, mentally and spiritually, leaving individuals in pain and frustration. They only add to your life's burdens. Motivators break down brick walls, manipulators build brick walls. Beware of manipulators.

I have accepted the fact that everyone will not accept my book. I'm cool with that. But I do know someone will understand my book and feel what I'm presenting in this book as well. My focus is finding individuals who see life as I see life, drawing them closer to me so we can fellowship by building a stronger foundation in our beliefs. This foundation we build makes us whole.

I was once asked the question, "What do you want the headlines to say when you are dead and gone?" For a minute I had to think about this question, true indeed it was a good one that I had never been asked before. So answering this question from the depths of my soul I'd say, "A humble man, a loving man, his life lives on".

I focus on becoming that humble and loving man each day I take breath, even when facing criticism for becoming humble and loving. I find myself at peace because I manage to always see the greater picture. That picture is spiritual happiness, the key to life.

You could not mix happiness and drama in life, it's to unbalanced so you won't succeed. Knowing this, I put in practice praying to God for the blessing to become a promising leader. Successfully receiving these gifts, I find myself blessed with other talents. Gratefully accepting these talents, I now see a greater life. In the words of Curtis Jackson, "This is God's plan homie, this ain't mine".

Evaluating more of myself, I think back to the day I realized I loved life. It was around the age of 24 for me, awakening in the early hours of the morning in my South Carolina home and hearing the birds chirping for the rising of the sun was near. As I approach nature, the clapping of trees from the whistling winds greets me. Everyday faces smile upon me, my friendship is worthy to be honored. I'm feeling similar to a prince turned king. Life is acknowledged and oh how I love it so much. In being thankful for my presence in this world, I realize that someone is not fortunate enough to have this privilege. The privilege of seeing your loved one's faces light up with joy after seeing you for the first time in quite some time. We know not the day or hour life may leave us and our soul claims it's rightful place. I cherish life as long as I have this life. There's a chance for my world to become stronger. Hungry for ambition and patient with prosperity. Life is a blessing, Life is earned, Life is given.

At one point, I became discouraged about finishing this book due to my insecurities. I felt handicapped about my purpose in life. Even the motivated ones need motivation at times, so I called my father and stated my discouragement to him. In wise words he said me, "What may be a dream to others is reality to you. People hear what you say, but everyone doesn't listen to what you say. In other words, most people only accept the right now instead of what's ahead in due time."

My father also stated, "Keep on with your blessing, for you are the one God has chosen to do his works. People will judge you and life will come at you in hard ways. As long as God provides this life for you, can't nothing or no one come between you and your work for God. He will see you through". In the words of Living Legend Sean Carter, "Sorry I'm a champion, you lost one".

Life is a hustle, and only the strongest survive. The William Lynch theory still exists today. Life is a game. A game played 24/7, 365 days a year, and you may take just a few water breaks. It's an individual sport, so you have no team help. There is no half time and no referees, just fearless opponents. There is only one rule to abide by, live! Once this game is over, you are retired for life. This game does have its advantages though. Sometimes you can make up for your mistakes, and as you get better in this game while reaching hall of fame status, there's a reward waiting for you at the end of your career.

So appreciate the small things in life. There may come a time where the small things in life are needed and not available to you. Honor the small things in life, because the small things in life prepare you for the finer things in life. Your short term goals adventure into your long term goals. Believe in evolution, it's the advancement of life. Knowing this, a transition is soon to come. Everyone will not be apart of this transition because everyone is not prepare for it. The individual who is secured will enjoy the changes in life.

As I complete this section of this book I leave you with this parable...Blood is thicker then water, but all nuts ain't dry. Sure as a man lives, sure as a man dies. They say, "Sky's the limit, but I can't touch the sky. Why ask the question, when the answer is in your eyes?"

Heaven

This story starts off when Mickey arrives to his home town (Belle Glade, Florida) on a nice summer afternoon, he hasn't been home in three years. He calls his best friend Lou to let him know he's in town.

Ring....Ring.... Lou answers the phone, still sleepy.

Lou: hello

Mickey: what they do boy?

Lou: who is this? Mickey this you, what up boy? What you calling me early this morning for, nigga are you crazy? I had to work last night, call me back later on.

Mickey: Nigga get your ass up, its 12 o'clock in the afternoon, I done touched down. I need you to ride with me somewhere. So be ready, I'll be there in 15 minutes. Be ready man.

They both hang up the phone.

15 minutes later Mickey pulls up to Lou's driveway, bumping his music loud in his new range rover. Mickey sitting in his truck, bouncing his head to the music. Lou, half dressed, comes outside and yells out to Mickey.

Lou: nigga turn that shit down, Tasha (Lou's girlfriend) in the house sleep! Come in, I have to finish getting ready. Lou goes back into his house.

Mickey, playing as if he didn't hear Lou, turns the music up louder and get out the truck and start dancing, a minute later he turns the music down and the truck off and walks in Lou's house. Lou is in the bathroom brushing his teeth, wakes Tasha up to let her know Mickey is in the living room and they are about to go off for a minute. Tasha gets up, walks into the living room and gives Mickey a hug and goes back into the bedroom to sleep more. Mickey, impatient, rushes Lou.

Mickey: man I told you to be ready nigga lets go, I'm not trying to be gone all day. I haven't seen my mama, brother or sister since I got to town. To be truthful they don't know I'm here yet.

Mickey walks back outside to his truck starts it up. Lou, with his belt in his hand and shirt on his shoulder, runs out the door yelling to Tasha to shut it and lock it. He hops in Mickey's truck and they pull off.

The Range Rover Ride

Mickey and Lou are headed through town on their way going to West Palm Beach to the mall to do a little shopping. As they ride through town Mickey stopped at P.D.Q., their favorite convenience store, to pick up some snacks and some blunts. "P.D.Q. is the one of the places in Belle Glade that will never change", Mickey says to himself. While in the store Mickey and Lou see a couple of their old classmates, Rob and Tim. As they greet one another, Rob tells Mickey and Lou about Keisha's party at club 81 that night. Mickey and Lou then pay for their things and then get back in the truck get on the highway and head to West Palm.

As Mickey gets on State Road 80 heading toward West Palm, Lou starts to role up a blunt. Mickey turns down the music to ask Lou what Mall is jumping.

Lou: Palm Beach Mall during this time of day, and it's summer time too? Man all type of women be in there.

Mickey with a smile on his face say's, "That's where we at then".

Lou: So how is your mother doing? When was the last time you talked to her?

Mickey: I talked to her about a week ago, I want to surprise her with a gift. That's why we going to the mall.

Lou: How are Ant, Sheka and Jason doing?

Mickey: They doin' alright. Ant got a football scholarship from Florida Atlantic. He leaves to report to camp Monday. Sheka and Jason about to have a baby, she is do in December. Nigga you should know more than me you live down here where they at.

The Question

Lou finish rolling up the blunt, looking for his lighter say to Mickey, "Nigga I been working third shift for two months straight, so you know I go straight to bed when I get home. On my off days I go to church and spend time with my lady".

Mickey: So you trying to live for The Lord now?

Lou: Man with all this shit going on round here like niggas getting drop like flies every time you go out, or turning on the news some crazy assed person doing some Ben Laden type of shit...Nigga you better call on God. Like the saying goes, "It ain't long as it has been". The Lord is about to soon come back. I want to be ready when he does.

Lou then finds his lighter, and lights the blunt.

Mickey: Nigga how are you going to talk about getting save and smoking weed or smoking period? Like my mama say, "Don't straddle the fence! If you going to live for God, do it right".

Lou: Mickey at least I'm trying, I don't want to be doing this all my life. I know The Lord going to deliver me from this wrong doing. I struggle everyday trying to be a sin free person, but I know if I continue to put forth effort doing good, eventually I will stop doing bad.

Lou passes the blunt to Mickey coughing saying to Mickey, "How are you going to talk about me when you don't even try to live for God? Tell me when was the last time you went to church and gave God some of your time?"

Mickey: Man I can't lie, it's been a minute since I stepped foot in a church. Man I know I need to pay God more attention, but I ain't ready for that lifestyle yet. I'm enjoying this one too much.

Lou: Ok Mickey, you better acknowledge God cuz I promise you that you are going to need him one day. Don't let it be said too late.

As Mickey passes the blunt back to Lou, Lou asks Mickey a personal question.

Lou: So tell me homie, how do you get your bread? I mean the last time I saw you, you was drivin' a bubble Chevy, wearing that old ass Nike watch you had since 9th grade. Now I see you and you looking clean. You got on a Rolex presidential watch on and you pushing an all black Range Rover sitting on 24's. Nigga tell me your story.

Mickey, with a puzzled look on his face, answers Lou.

Mickey: I knew you were going to ask me that question sooner or later. Well it all started like this. One day I was sitting in my dorm room just chillin' and this nigga I use to chill with named Taylor Made came to holla at me. I hadn't seen this nigga in a minute. Man I tell you this nigga use to be a bum! Head stayed nappy and had no hoes to save his life. But when I saw this nigga again homeboy was iced out, had a fresh cut, some tight J's on his feet and one of the baddest bitches I ever seen in my life. I can't front, homeboy looked and smelled like money.

Mickey: So I was like "Nigga you eatin' and I know that bullshit degree ain't doing it for you". So I said, "Man put your boy on, I want to eat to!" Taylor Made starts grinning and he says, "Nigga you ain't ready for this type of lifestyle. Nigga I push major weight, I'm almost at king pen status. You won't last in these streets, you too soft."

Mickey: The nigga underestimated me because I'm cool and stay to myself, but after constantly asking this nigga he finally put me on. He starts me out with a pound of green. I went to getting off so fast because my face was so gator with in months, I went from pushin' a pound of weed a week to 200 hundred pounds a month. I was making all type of bread. Word got out that I was getting off weight so fast 'til this big time coke dealer by the name of Meko, some Spanish motherfucker from Spain, got in touch with me and started supplying me with coke. At first I didn't want to sale coke, I was making good money with the weed, but we all know coke is where the real money at and the money really started talking to me.

Mickey: Man Meko put me on and I had coke flooding the streets of Atlanta. I could push 75 keys of coke in two days. It got so bad to people started calling me, "Heaven". My shit is guaranteed to take you to that higher place. But it's not all good. I have to watch my back twenty four seven, even the niggas who work for me can't be trusted. This nigga Taylor Made wants my head because I won't give him my connect and I got more street credit than he did. This crooked assed police officer by the name E-Bo wants me dead because I don't respect him. Man I face a lot of bullshit, and I guess you reap what you sow.

Lou passes the blunt back to Mickey saying...

Lou: You said had...What are you doing with the dope game now? You need to stop Mickey, it's not you. I remember Mickey Blade as the number one High School All American football player in the country who never touch a drug in his life. Now he's one of America's top gangsters. What has this world come to?

Mickey: Man I know, that's one of my main reasons for coming home. I had to get away from all the drama and fame going on in my playground. I want to give it up, but the money keeps calling me. Besides playing football, which I can't do anymore do to my career ending injury, the only thing I know how to do is this lifestyle I live now. One day I will stop it but now I don't think I can.

Lou: Man you can do what ever you put your mind to. Mickey you are a smart person, what do you mean you can't do anything else besides selling drugs? I know this is not Mr. Honors Society talking? Man you have a bright future ahead of you, now you just fuckin' it up. Just put it in God's hands, he will see you through.

Mickey: Man God knows what's going on, I don't have to tell him. Anyway Lou, this information I shared with you, don't tell nobody.

Lou cuts Mickey off. "What you mean man? Your business is your business and I really don't want any parts of it."

Mickey: You heard what I said, don't tell nobody. I already have enough shit going on in my life, I don't need more drama.

Lou: I feel you, I won't tell nobody. Now let me hit the blunt before it goes out.

The Lady In Palm Beach Mall

After a 30 minute drive from Belle Glade Mickey and Lou arrive to the Palm Beach Mall. Excited to see the mall, Mickey tells Lou to get what he wants. As they enter the mall Mickey notices this beautiful black woman that he feels he has to approach. Lou's mind is on a new pair of Jordan's that are displayed in the window of a shoe store.

Mickey walks behind the young lady constantly saying, "Excuse me....Hey miss now I know you hear me talking to you." The young lady finally stops turns around and says with a rushing attitude, "What do you want sir? I'm trying to get out of this mall. I have somewhere to be at the moment". Mickey introduces himself to lady as Mickey Blade and she introduces herself to him as Ms. Nayia Shine.

Mickey: How are you doing Ms. Shine?

Nayia: I'm fine

Mickey: Well I know you said you need to be getting somewhere, so I won't prolong your time. I must say I find you attractive and I want to get to know you, if it's not asking too much.

Nayia: I don't know about that, you see I have a lot going on in my life at the moment dealing with school and living a God fearing life. I really just want to stay on track. Sorry, but you have a nice day.

Nayia, proceeds to the exit door of the mall. Mickey is impressed from the way she tells him no so he runs behind her, getting her attention once more. As they walk to Ms Nayia's car Mickey expresses to her how everything happens for a reason, and how she can be a help in his life and he just wants to start off as friends. Ms Nayia finally gives in and tells Mickey to give her his phone number and she will think about calling him. Mickey happily gives her the number and she accepts it by putting it in her cell phone. Afterwards she gets into her car and drives off.

Mickey walks back into the mall to reconnect with Lou. After spending about 3 hour's shopping Mickey and Lou finally leave the mall and head back to Belle Glade. Before heading back to Belle Glade Mickey stops at a gas station to gas up his truck. It's almost dark and Mickey doesn't like being out at night with out his gun on him, which he realizes he does have on him at the time. As soon as he gets out of the truck a beat up car rapidly pulls up and two jack boys jump out pointing choppers at Mickey and Lou, yelling at them.

Jack Boy 1: Fuck boy give it up!

Mickey looks at Lou and tells him to just get out of the truck and be cool. As they proceed to get out of the truck, one of the jack boys with the chopper pointed at Mickey says...

Jack Boy 1: Nigga don't I know you? You Mickey Blade! I remember you scored 4 touchdowns against my high school Sun Coast. Nigga you was that deal. So, who you play for now?

Mickey, thinking of a quick lie, said "The Dallas Cowboys. I'm just home for the off season."

Jack Boy 1: Homeboy we going to let you go on good face, but you better ride with your fire or stay your ass home. This is a chopper zone!

The Jack Boys hop back in their car and zoom off. Mickey and Lou, at first scared, now laugh and joke about their encounter that just took place as they gas up. Mickey promises himself to never, ever forget his gun again...no matter where he goes. They then pull off from the gas station, next stop Belle Glade.

Home Sweet Home (Mama's House)

Mickey and Lou return back to Belle Glade after spending all day shopping at the mall in West Palm Beach. Before taking Lou home, Mickey stops at his mother's house to see his family who he hasn't seen in 3 years. Mickey pulls up in his mother's driveway. She was laying across the couch near the front room window, drinking her favorite tea and listening to some gospel music. She hears a loud rattling from some music outside in her yard. Ms. Mae pulls back the curtains from the window to see who it was that was making loud noise in her driveway. She notices her son, who she hasn't seen in three years, getting out of a truck. She rushed to the front door with tears in her eye, a hug and kiss waiting for her son as he approached her with excitement.

Ms. Mae: Oh my God my long lost son. It's good to see you. Thank you Jesus for bringing my baby home.

Mickey drops his bags and hugs his mother with a smile on his face, saying "It's good to see you too Mama". Along with Lou, who greets Ms. Mae with a hug as well, they all walk into the house. Inside of the house Mickey was surprised by his younger, 4 month pregnant sister Sheka, along with her husband Jason and their youngest sibling Ant.

Everyone is located in the living room, the family's favorite place the house. After everyone greets each other Mickey gives everyone their gift he bought for them at the mall. Everyone enjoys their gift that Mickey bought them. Mickey's mother Ms. Mae asks Mickey a couple of questions...

Ms. Mae: Whose truck are you driving? And how you get all this money to buy these nice things you have for us? Not to mention I haven't seen you in 3 years and you haven't finished College? Still you come home with all this? Something ain't right! Tell me what's going on Mickey. (Mickey silent).

Ms. Mae: Boy I know you hear me talking to you. I hope you ain't doing anything that's displeasing to God. You know God don't like ugly.

Mickey hugs his mother again kissing her on the side of her face saying jokingly, "Well God must love me then mama, because I ain't ugly".

Everyone begins to laugh at Mickey's joke.

Ms. Mae: Get off me boy with your silly self. God ain't crazy about pretty either.

Mickey: I ain't pretty either, you can call me so fresh and so clean.

Ms. Mae: You just better not be doing nothing you ain't got no business doing. I raised you better then that.

Mickey: I know Mama, but I didn't come home to argue with you. I came home to enjoy my family and friends and get away from the political world I find success in.

Ms Mae: Nigga please, you can talk all educated and highly incorporated all you want to, like I said, "You better not be doing anything you ain't got no business doing."

Ms. Mae then leaves the living room area goes into her bedroom to snuggle up in her bed and read her bible.

Lou then reminds Mickey about the party that night at club 81, so he needs to go home to freshen up for it. Mickey gets ready for the party before taking Lou home to freshen up. 45 minutes later, dressed up in his laid back gear, Mickey tells his family bye and he will see them in the morning because he's about to hang out for the remainder of the night. He then takes Lou home to get ready and off to the party they go.

It's Good to be Home

It's around 10 o'clock that Saturday night at club 81. Mickey and Lou walk up from the parking lot to the front of the remodeled club (still the same old club to Mickey). Everyone in the parking lot was so amazed to see him. He received all type of hugs and hand shakes, and occasionally someone will ask him to let them hold something (money). Made Mickey feel warm inside, he then realizes he was a home town legend. Mickey then proceeded to enter the loud club.

Mickey and Lou walk into the club and the DJ spots Mickey and gives him a shot out. Family and friends in the club greets him. After a while getting reacquainted with everyone he notices his closer friends waiting in the quieter corner of the club with Lou mingling. Mickey was reunited with his friends.

Mickey greets them with, "What they do ya'll?" He gives all his closest homeboys and home girls hugs and dap. Mickey wants to buy the bar out, but the promoter of Keisha's party beat Mickey to it. So after hours of sitting in the club smoking and drinking, laughing and joking, Mickey's and his friends exit to the club parking lot to get fresh air and wait on the club to end. Mickey's drunken friend RJ, staggering out of the club, burst out amongst the friends.

RJ: Mickey what you know about this big time king pin in Atlanta? The word is that this nigga got the streets on lock in the "A". They call him "Heaven!"

Mickey looked as if he was interested, but didn't know much about what RJ was talking about.

Mickey: Yea man, it's wild up there. All I do is go to work and home. I try to limit myself from the streets of Atlanta. Tell me though, "How did you hear about this king pin down hear in Florida?

RJ: Homeboy the streets travel, just like it has ears and eyes. Anything that takes place in the streets it's known across the world. The streets got it's own mind and soul.

Lou walks toward Mickey and RJ conversation.

Lou jokingly says to RJ, "Nigga shut the hell up with your drunk ass! Mickey lets go get something to eat at Carlyle Café before it get crowded."

Mickey, with a puzzled look on his face after hear what RJ told him, gets in his truck along with Lou and they go gets something to eat at Carlyle's. Mickey takes Lou home afterwards. Right before Lou gets out of the truck and called it a night Mickey asks Lou a question.

Mickey: Lou did you hear RJ talk about this nigga "Heaven" running the streets of Atlanta? I wonder who this nigga is? When I get back in Atlanta I'm going to look for this nigga and tell him to put me on if he eating like that! (Mickey laughs out loud)

Lou comments drunkenly...

Lou: Man I don't want to hear that shit right now. I got a hang over, I know Tasha is going to trip because I came home too late and I have to wake up at 11 in the morning to go to church tomorrow.

That reminds me, you should come to church with me and Tasha in the morning.

Mickey, with no intention of going to church tells Lou, "Just call me in the morning when you get up".

Lou says, "Ok." He exits Mickey's truck and goes into his house while Mickey pulls off to go home (Mama's house).

Farewell Home

After spending a week visiting old friends and family it's the following Sunday afternoon and Mickey decides to hit the park up before heading back to Atlanta in the morning. Enjoying the music, the homies showing off their custom made cars and his people having a good time Mickey receives a call on his cell phone from Ms. Shines.

Mickey: Hello?

Nayia: Yes, may I speak to Mickey please?

Mickey remembers her voice...

Mickey: How are you doing Ms. Nayia? I didn't expect for you to call me.

Nayia: I'm blessed and I was free so I decided to give you a call since you crossed my mind.

Mickey: Oh really? That's good to hear. So, wuzz up?

Mickey and Ms. Nayia talk about their college life and where they are originally from. Just as soon as Ms. Nayia asks Mickey what he do for a living Ms. Nayia gets a beep on her cell phone and has to continue the conversation at a later time. Mickey goes back to enjoying the excitement of the park.

After that the police run everybody away from the park. When it gets dark everyone usually goes to Eve's Ave to the loading ramp to mingle or just chill along that whole street. Basically the party is brought from the park to the streets. Since Mickey has been home, he has seen all type of crazy stuff. Crack heads performing dances in the middle of traffic and the homies stunning in their cars. Mickey says to himself, "Only in Belle Glade". As Mickey cruises through the Strip in his Range Rover he spots Lou chillin' on the loading ramp. He pulls over to holla at Lou.

Mickey: Lou what's up?

Lou: Man, I thought you were gone back to the "A"?

Mickey: Naw, I'm leaving in the morning. I wonder if you wanted to come back with me for a little vacation just to get away for a minute.

Lou: You have perfect timing because we just got a week off from my job and Tasha is going to this church convention for women in Texas for a week. I don't know about going to Atlanta with you. You living a pretty hectic life up there and I don't need that type of drama in my life, I'm doing too good.

Mickey: Man I ain't gonna to let nothing happen to you. I promise you a good and safe time with no drama. Come on dawg, come back with your boy.

Lou, thinking about Mickey's proposal, says "I don't know about that dawg, just hit me up in the morning before you get on the road".

Mickey: Well I'm about to go to the crib and get my self straight for tomorrow. I'll hit you up in the morning.

Mickey goes to his mother's house and gets himself prepared for his trip back to the A.

It's morning and Mickey is packing all his things in his truck with his mother in his ear about living right and driving back to Atlanta safe. Lou calls and tells Mickey that he decided to take him up on his offer about going to Atlanta. Mickey finished packing his bags in his truck and hugged his mother. After she prays for him he picks Lou up and Atlanta bound they are.

Range Rover Ride 2

Mickey and Lou are on the Interstate 75 heading north to Atlanta. With his arm hanging out the window, bouncing his head to the music and smoking a black and mild Lou turns the music down and asks Mickey a question he has been wanting to know the answer to for a while.

Lou: Mickey, I'm curious about how you operate your illegal business without getting caught up by the law.

Mickey looked Lou into his eyes and says, "It's strictly business and never pleasure for me. I keep a very low profile and I don't hang around with no one I work with, or go to the same places where someone I know hangs. To be honest I don't even hang out in Atlanta period, I travel to have me time. This weekend I have this big thing at my club we got to go to. As far as how I get my money, it goes like this...

Mickey: I don't do phones, I have people to do that for me. Whenever a shipment is needed a code is passed around through 50 different phone calls. Only the dealer and the buyer understand the code words, this lets the dealer know how much the buyer is willing to spend and how many people are with them on the transaction and location. Any information needed is provided by the code, and all of my workers are trained to carry themselves professionally at all times during work hours. It's a job and that how I treat it.

Lou: So what part do you play in the business?

Mickey: I fund the whole operation. You can pretty much call me Blade's Bank of America because I touch nothing but money. I make a personal visit with my connect and have my deliverer men take the shipment to my warehouses outside of Georgia. From the warehouse my workers on the streets are supplied. I keep my warehouse packed with keys of coke so I probably place an order 3 times a year.

Mickey: I only have 250,000 in the bank, which is the money I make a year from my club. I have someone running as well. The money I make from the streets is safely hidden in a place where only I and God know. The only thing I do is pay my taxes, make sure my connect and operation is good, sit back and collect bread.

Lou proudly says to Mickey, "I have one more question. Well, I have two more questions? You said you can get off 75 keys of coke in two days. How much money is that?"

Mickey well one key cost 20,000 dollars so it's around 1.5 million in two days, 5 million a week and in a month...well you do the math.

Lou: Damn dawg! I could imagine. Now tell me, "How much money you sitting on?"

Mickey laughing says just as much money you sitting on. Nigga that ain't none of your business how much money I got.

Lou: Ahh.... Fuck nigga! Keep it to yourself then fuck boy.

They both laugh as they continue their trip to Atlanta.

Welcome to the A.

After riding for nine hours, occasionally stopping for gas and food, Mickey and Lou finally made it to Atlanta. Before going to Mickey's home that's outside of Atlanta Mickey gives Lou a tour of Atlanta's city life. Impressed by the sites of Atlanta, Lou tells Mickey, "I see why you stayed in Atlanta for so long, this is where it's at".

Stopping at the gas station to get some blunts Mickey runs into a face he doesn't want to see... Detective Leroy Brown A.K.A. E-BO.

E-Bo, talking with a evil smile, says "If it ain't Mickey Blade or should I say the famous 'Heaven'".

Mickey, with a slight unit on his face says "Wuzz up E-Bo, what do you want?"

E-Bo gets in Mickey face saying, "You know what I want motherfucker, I want my cut".

Mickey: Man I don't know what you talking about. I don't owe anybody anything.

E-Bo: Oh yeah? You gonna pay me nigga, don't nothing come through these streets and I don't get my piece of the pie. My patience has run out with you nigga. I'm going get what I want one way or the other motherfucker. Don't make me come to your house nigga, because that will be the last time you see that motherfucker.

Mickey with a smile on his face says to E-Bo, "Motherfucker you going to stop playing with me before the police department of Atlanta find you way out in Arizona. When they do find you, well, let's just say you will not look the same as now. You know you can't touch me so why try? Now if you don't mind I need to run in here to grab some blunts so I can smoke. I got that good green too, you want to buy some?"

Mickey, laughing, continues to go into the gas station, as E-Bo yells out of rage to Mickey, "In due time you gonna get what's coming to you nigga. You may need to tell your family to get ready to dress in all black because they going to need it for your ass real soon and that's a promise!" E-Bo gets in his undercover car and speeds off.

When Mickey returns to the truck after buying some blunts, Lou who was waiting in the truck when the encounter takes place ask, "Mickey was that E-Bo who you was talking to?" Mickey replied, "Yes, how did you know that?"

Lou: Nigga I know an undercover police when I see one. I can tell by his car and them dark ass tints on his window.

Mickey, laughing, says "I got black ass tints on my window, I ain't the police."

Lou: Man you always got something smart to say, you know what I'm talk about damnit!

Mickey: I'm just playing witcha.

After leaving the gas station, Mickey finally arrives to his house. Lou walks in the house and was speechless, Mickey ask Lou what does he think of his crib, Lou answered, "Man this is something I never dream of staying in, you doin' it dawg". After introducing Lou to the whole house the both of them freshen up from the long day they had and call it a night. While smoking a blunt Mickey walks into the living room where Lou was sitting on the couch quietly reading his bible.

Mickey: You want to hit this weed dawg?

Lou: Naw, man I'm in the word right now.

Mickey sits on the couch next to Lou saying, "What you reading?"

Lou: I'm just going over some different chapters the pastor told me to read on.

Mickey: Oh, well do you that cuz I'm about to go to bed. I need rest.

Just as Mickey was about to leave and go to his bedroom Lou ask Mickey a question, "What do you think heaven is like"?

Mickey, with smoke coming from his mouth says, "I believe it's beautiful, probably the most beautiful place eyes ever seen. Too bad the way I'm going I won't be there to see it."

Lou: Why is it so hard for you to give God a chance? You see the life I live is not perfect but I try to live right Mickey, you can too.

Mickey, standing in the doorway of the living room says to Lou, "Man let me tell you something. All my life I have been good. Like you said to me I never drink, I never smoke, I was good to my mother and Belle Glade. But that day I lost my so called promising future I stop trusting in God and started putting my faith in self. So far, so good. Now don't get me wrong I know God and hopefully someday may have a relationship with Him but until then it's all about me.

Mickey then leaves the living room and goes to bed. Lou, in a low sorrowful voice says, "Lord, bless Mickey's soul." Then Lou continues to read his bible.

Meeting with the Boss

The next morning Mickey gets himself prepared for his day. Dressed in his business attire, he goes into the guest room to wake Lou up.

Mickey: Lou get up, we have a long day a head of us

Lou still sleepy asks, "Where are we going?"

Mickey: Man just get up and get ready. Mickey leaves Lou to get ready and returns to the kitchen to finish cooking them breakfast. An hour later Lou walks into the kitchen ready for the day. As he sits down at the dining table, Lou ask Mickey, why you all dressed up and where are we going today?

Mickey brings his plate of breakfast to the table and says to Lou, "You remember that nigga John Jackson who used to hang with us in middle school?" Lou tells Mickey that the name sounds familiar but he would have to see dude.

Mickey: The nigga who we use to call John John...

Lou shakes his head because he still can't put the face with the name

Mickey: Well I ran into him about a year ago he said he had been living here in Atlanta every since his family left Belle Glade. He asked about you, so I thought I would take you over to his crib and chill with him for a minute while I go take care of some business. I won't be gone longer then a couple of hours.

An hour later Mickey and Lou arrive at John John's house. Lou then tells Mickey he does remember dude soon as John John opens the door. While John John and Lou get reacquainted, Mickey tells them both that he will be back in a couple of hours. Lou and John John tell Mickey they're good and proceed into the house. Mickey gets back into his truck and drives to his destination.

After riding for about 3 hours, Mickey makes it's to his connect's meeting place. After Mickey is patted down by tight security he walks to the swimming pool area where his connect was relaxing in a lounge chair, smoking a Cuban cigar.

Meko: It's my buddy Heaven, "How are you doing today"?

Mickey, with a unhappy look displayed on his face, tells Meko "I'm doing fine. Here's your money. Count it, it's all there.

Meko: I have known you for sometime now, you have the right amount I trust you. But Heaven, what is troubling you? Tell me.

Mickey expresses himself to Meko saying, "Naw, its something that my cousin asked me last night that's been on my mind all day. I keep having run ins with these niggas threatening me, which they just fronting, and I'm starting to have a change of heart about the life I live.

Meko gets up from his seat and tells Mickey to walk with him.

Meko: From the first time I met you I said to myself, "What is this kid doing?" Heaven you are a good man. I never see you mad or even disrespectful, the streets they love you, people love you, but Heaven now its time for you to love yourself. I know you may say who am I to talk about going good, but you see I used to be good a long time ago. It's too late for me but you have bright future. So, maybe it is time for you to change your line of work. You think about what I said Heaven.

Mickey took some strong thought about his life after having a conversation with Meko. After leaving Meko's spot Mickey goes back to John John's house to hang out with Lou and John John. As Mickey walked to the living room where Lou and John John were on the Playstation, Mickey tells Lou that before he takes him back to Florida they are going to church that Sunday morning.

Lou surprisingly says, "I know you ain't talking about going to church. Lord, what done got into him?"

Mickey: You was right, I got to give God a try. I'm willing to try anything that's going to make me a better person. I know God's a start.

John John then tells Mickey and Lou about a church that he attends in Atlanta, maybe they should give it a visit. Lou and Mickey agree.

Ms. Nayia in the A.

Night has fallen and Mickey and Lou are back at Mickey's house lounging. Mickey receives a call on his cell phone from Ms. Nayia. Mickey answers.

Mickey: How are you doing Ms. Nayia?

Ms. Nayia: I'm blessed and yourself?

Mickey: I can't complain.

Ms. Nayia and Mickey get into a conversation, and finally Ms. Nayia goes back to the question she asked Mickey from the last conversation, "What do you do for a living?" Mickey tells Ms. Nayia he owns a successful nightclub in Atlanta. Ms. Nayia, stereotyping Mickey, says when she meet him she thought he was a drug dealer but it's good to see that he has something good going for himself. Most men she runs into are drug dealers and she just won't accept that lifestyle that she grow up in. Mickey, at a silence, feels ashamed because she is talking about him as one of those guys she normally meets. He wants to tell her but he didn't due to fear of losing her friendship.

Changing the subject Ms. Nayia then tells Mickey her profession. She's a nurse and was calling Mickey to let him know she's in Atlanta for a work convention until Sunday. Maybe they could meet Saturday so Mickey can show her the city of Atlanta. She was only there for business and never got to see the city.

Mickey, excited, tells Ms. Nayia about the special event he's hosting at his nightclub and he will love for her to accompany him along with his cousin Lou to the special event.

After saying no for many different reasons, Ms. Nayia finally said yes to Mickey's continuous begging but under one condition. Ms. Nayia stated, "When I say I'm ready to go, it's time to go." Mickey agrees to her verbal contract. Mickey then tells Ms. Nayia Saturday morning he will come to her hotel to pick her up. "See you then, Nubian Queen." Ms.

Nayia smiles while saying bye as they both hang up the phone, ending their conversation.

Lenox Mall

Saturday has come. Mickey, Lou, and Ms. Nayia are at the Lenox Mall ready to shop, preparing themselves for the party at Mickey's club Punchierilla. As soon as Mickey and his small entourage walks into the mall people swarm Mickey, questioning him about the event that's taking place at his club that night.

After talking to different people about the party, Mickey and Lou go to get a hair cut at the barber shop in the mall, while Ms. Nayia goes shopping for some heels to match her evening gown. She tells Mickey and Lou that she will meet them back at the barber shop and proceeded to the shoe store.

After sitting in the barber shop for little over an hour, laughing and joking with the barbers, Mickey calls Ms. Nayia to tell her to meet him and Lou at the food court. As soon as Mickey and Lou exit the barber shop Mickey runs into another one of his arch enemies, Taylor Made.

Taylor Made, with his small entourage, says to Mickey...

Taylor Made: What's up boy? I haven't seen you in a minute. Where you been hiding at?

Mickey looks as if his day was badly wounded after seeing Taylor Made,

Mickey: I been around, so what's up?

Taylor Made: You know what's up. When you gonna to let me get that connect?

Mickey: Homeboy you know I don't fuck with you like that. Besides, I've taken another route in life, and if I was still doing my thing I wasn't giving you shit. So if you and your people don't mind, me and my people will be on our way.

Noticing, Ms. Nayia coming towards the small occasion Mickey and Lou walks towards her. Taylor Made Grabs Mickey's shoulder saying arguably,

Taylor Made: Nigga I made you. If it wasn't for me shorty you wouldn't be shit in these streets, pussy boy. You owe me nigga, so pay your maker or meet that motherfucker.

Lou is cursing Taylor Made out about touching Mickey as Taylor Made's entourage disputes with Lou. Mickey tells Lou to chill, he got it under control. While removing Taylor Made's hand from his shoulder Mickey says to Taylor Made...

Mickey: Nigga don't you never put your hands on me again. Like I told the last nigga that threatened me, don't let me have your ass missing. Face it, I'm better then you at your own game. I get more love in your city than you do. Now I know you wish you were me and you are not the only one. Many people wish they could wear my shoes. Sorry to tell you, these shoes are custom made only for me.

As Mickey walks away from the occasion with Lou to reconnect with Ms. Nayia Taylor Made yells out,

"Nigga don't think you can't be touch, you and your punk ass homeboy whoever he is. Y'all niggas dead and that's real talk!" Taylor Made and entourage then exit the mall. Coming toward the end of the dispute, Ms. Nayia ask Mickey what was the problem? Mickey tells her just some haters hating, nothing serious to worry about. They continue to enjoy their day at the mall.

SO FRESH, SO CLEAN

The time has finally come, and Mickey is so excited about the party at his club Punchierilla. He's stepping out in his all cream three piece Taylor Made suit with his light brown Stacey Adam's designer shoes with matching brim. He's got his new custom made diamond Rolex shining on his wrist along with the diamonds in his eye glasses, and he's smelling like Sean "Puffy" Combs "Unforgivable". He's waiting for Lou in his white on white custom made Range Rover.

Lou is exiting Mickey's house in his all white linen formal wear, with dark brown Stacey Adam's shoes and matching brim. He tells Mickey as he enters the truck, "I must admit, you the man." Mickey replied to Lou by saying, "You look like a boss yourself." Mickey then pulls off to pick up Ms. Nayia from her hotel.

Thirty minutes later they arrive at Ms. Nayia's hotel, who's waiting patiently in front in her all white designer evening gown with the matching heels that she runway walked into Mickey's truck. Her hair lay perfectly flat falls to her back displaying only natural beauty.

The most beautiful creation Mickey has ever laid eyes on thought Mickey, gazing at her beauty. Mickey is speechless. Ms. Nayia tells Mickey and Lou how good they look and smell as she enters the truck. Mickey and Lou address her the same way. They all smile with confidence as Mickey pulls off from the hotel heading to Club Punchierilla.

A Sad Night To Remember

Arriving to club Punchierilla, looking glamorous, Mickey and entourage enter the club. The place is packed with everyone dressed in their finest, smelling good, and looking good, club Punchierilla is the place to be.

Mickey and entourage are escorted to their seats in front of the live performance that's taking place on the crafted design stage. Ms. Nayia tells Mickey that he has a nice set up, it reminds her of "Ray's Boom Boom Room" from the movie "Life". Mickey, smiles as Lou makes his comment about the club.

Lou: Yeah this will be the type of place Al Capone and all the other big time gangsters back in day would come to. Nigga who you think you are, a Don?

Mickey laughs as they all enjoy the singing and live bands that perform at Club Punchierilla.

Meanwhile, on the other side of Atlanta, Taylor Made and E-Bo met up to plot on killing "Heaven".

Taylor Made: Man E-Bo, this nigga Heaven got to die. As long as this nigga still taking breaths, I can't comin' up like I need to. It's time for this nigga to go.

E-Bo, with a sinister look on his face tells Taylor Made, "Before we discuss anything, nigga you got my money?"

Taylor Made hands over the back pack full of money. E-Bo, with a evil smile on his face, says "Now we can talk."

E-Bo: I'm tired of this motherfucker myself, fuck all this being patient shit. I want this nigga dead tonight and since he's your creation, you handle him.

Taylor made with an Evil unit on his face just waiting on the word from E-Bo to kill heaven says "consider that nigga already dead".

Now back at the club Mickey and his friends are enjoying themselves, but it's getting late and Ms. Nayia has to get back to the hotel to prepare herself for her flight back to West Palm Beach tomorrow. Mickey and Lou have to get some rest for church in the morning and their ride back to Florida as well.

Finally leaving the club after shaking folks's hands and thanking everyone for coming out tonight to his event, Mickey proceeds to take Ms. Nayia to her hotel. He and Lou head to his house to prepare for their long day tomorrow.

Arriving to Ms. Nayia's hotel, Mickey gets out of his truck to walk Ms. Nayia to her room. He leaves Lou in the truck running after telling him he will be back shortly. Lou and Ms. Nayia exchange goodbyes as Mickey and Ms. Nayia continue to the entrance of the hotel.

At Ms. Nayia's room door Ms. Nayia tells Mickey she had a wonderful time. She gives Mickey a hug and continues to enter her room. Mickey then states, "That's it? When can I see you again?"

Ms. Nayia, halfway in her door, turns around and looks Mickey straight in his face and says, "Mickey you are a good person and will probably make some lady the happiest woman in the world, just not me. I don't know why, but my soul doesn't agree with you. Physically I want you, really I do, but my spirit just won't let me. I'm sorry Mickey, but move on with your life. We can't be together."

She leans over and kisses Mickey on the side of his face, enters her room and closes her door.

Mickey, smiling, says to himself as he walks back to his truck, "She's mine, in due time."

Mickey, exiting the hotel, hears a familiar voice. "I told you, nigga, I was going to get your ass!" Shots goes off, bum...bum...bum...Mickey dives to the floor of the hotel along with other people, then quickly jumps up with his gun in hand realizing he left Lou in the running truck.

Coming outside the hotel to a Range Rover full of bullet holes and his cousin Lou hanging out of the passenger side badly bleeding, he notices a black car speeding off from the crime scene.

Mickey quickly puts Lou back into the truck gets on the drivers side and rushes Lou to the nearest hospital.

Mickey with tears in his eyes says to Lou...

Mickey: Cuzo, hold on we almost to the hospital!

Lou, in serious pain and barely alive, coughing up blood from his mouth says to Mickey...

Lou: Cuzo, you still going to church tomorrow?

Tears then really start to run out of Mickey's eyes as he tells Lou...

Mickey: Of course you're going too.

Tears begins to run Lou eyes as he tells Mickey,

Lou: Naw Cuzo, I don't think I going to make tomorrow's service, but tell the preacher to pray for me. Mickey, remember me asking you "What do you think heaven is like?"

Mickey: Yes, but don't talk like that we almost to the hospital.

In a sad, slow voice Lou tells Mickey, "Cuzo I'm going to see what heaven is like. I think I will probably see Tupac and Biggie. That's probably who I will be hanging with the most. I'll tell them you say what's up." Mickey laughs as Lou continues to speak while blood drips from his wounded body, spattered all over Mickey's white interior in his

Range Rover. Five minutes away from the nearest hospital, Lou speaks his final words.

Lou: Cuzo, promise me you will start going to church and give God some of your time. At least give him a chance, he'll work things out for you. I believe he will, but you have to believe he will also.

Mickey: I promise Cuzo.

Lou: That's good. Well Cuzo I'm getting sleepy, wake me up when we get to the hospital.

Lou, with a smile on his face, closes his eyes never to open them again.

With tears constantly running down Mickey's face he is repeatedly saying, "Lou get up, we almost there! Lou wake up!" It's now too late, Lou is dead.

It's So Hard To Say Goodbye

After a long and painful week, Mickey returns to Belle Glade after shipping Lou's body back to the hometown funeral home. Lou's funeral took place at the high school he attended on a sad Saturday morning. Friends and family members were all there to pay their last respects to their home going loved one, James Louis.

Mickey didn't attend Lou's funeral, he couldn't stand to see the face of his best friend lying there in that casket on the account of his wrong doing. Instead, Mickey spends the whole day at the old dike, where he and Lou use to go fishing during their younger days growing up in Belle Glade.

At the dike, watching seabirds snatch fish from the huge lake, tears run down Mickey's face as he thinks about the entire drama that's taken place in his life. The one person he trusted is now gone, never to see him again. Missing several calls from concerned family and friends, Mickey finally answers his cell phone after noticing it was Meko calling him at the present time.

Mickey answers his phone with a sad voice. Tears yet running his face...

Mickey: What up Meko?

Meko: How are you doing Heaven? I called you to say sorry about what happened to your friend. How are you holding up?

Mickey: Man I'm good. I'm just sitting here at the old dike where I and Lou use to go fishing when we were kids. I'm trying to clear my mind from all this madness going on in my life.

Meko: I see. Well you know Mickey we all must die one day, but important the thing about death is to die happy. Leaving this world at peace is the greatest gift a man can possess. From knowing you, your friend was a pretty good man as well, I'm pretty sure he died happy.

Mickey listens with nothing to say as Meko ends the conversation.

Meko: Well Mickey, it's nice doing business with you. I consider you as a friend, more like a brother from another mother, you know?

Mickey laughs.

Meko: Your problems in Atlanta will soon be over. Take care my friend.

Staying in a hotel in West Palm Beach, the next morning Mickey decides to go to the church he grew up in back in Belle Glade. Dressed in a black pin striped suit with the blacks gators on his feet, his Sunday's finest, Mickey visits Lou's grave before going to church.

Mickey exits his Range Rover at the grave site as the sky becomes dark, the wind begins to blow and it starts to rain. As Mickey approached the tombstone that his best friend lied six feet under, his throat becomes numb and his soul is troubled with pain. Staring at Lou's grave brings tears from his eyes.

Speechless, Mickey feels he must still express his self to Lou.

Mickey: What's up dawg? First I must say sorry for not making your funeral yesterday. To be honest with you, I could not stand to see you lying there in that box like that. (Mickey pauses for a second) Man words can't express how sorry I am for your death. I know you would probably say it was your time to go, but if it wasn't for me you would still be here.

I know who killed you and I want revenge so bad, but constantly hearing your voice in my ear telling me to "leave it alone" and "let it be" is the only reason why I won't go after them niggas. I'm done with the streets, yeah that's it for me. I'm just mad it took for this to happen for me to see the bigger picture.

I'm think I'm going to take your advice and start going to church. I'm headed on my way there after I leave here. You were right, I need to give God some of my time, He's really been good to me. It's time for me to be good to Him. Well I need to be heading to church, I just wanted to stop by and say what's up. I'll be visiting you often. Oh yeah, tell Tupac and Biggie to let your boy get a copy of their new CD before it hit the streets. I know both of them are coming out with another one soon. Well I got to ride Cuzo, I love you man.

As Mickey walks away from Lou's grave the rain stops and the sun begins to shine. Mickey, with little relief from the conversation with Lou, gets in his truck and heads to his church.

Arriving at the church he hesitates about entering the old, small building he once called his second home. From the outside you hear the church family worshiping and praising God. Mickey takes a deep breath and enters the old church. Walking inside his sister and brother-in-law notice and greet him with a hug. His mother, sitting in the front of the church with tears in her eyes, thanks God to see her son in the house of the Lord. Mickey, with tears in his eyes, walks to the head of the church while the preacher is preaching. He bows down on his knees at the altar and says loudly to the congregation, "Somebody pray for me."

Amen

Printed in the United States
102518LV00001B/37-165/P

9 780978 743970